The Childhood of Jesus

Retold by
Christopher Rawson
and The Revd. R. H. Lloyd
Chaplain of the Dragon School, Oxford

Illustrated by
Victor Ambrus

Nihil obstat Anton Cowan *Censor*
Imprimatur The Rt. Rev. David Konstant, V.G., M.A.,

Nearly two thousand years ago, Palestine, the homeland of the Jews, was part of the huge Roman Empire.

The Roman Emperor Augustus had appointed Herod, a cruel man, to be the ruler of the Jews. But Herod was not a Jew and the Jews would not accept him as their king.

The Jews believed that God had promised their ancestor Abraham, many centuries before, that he had chosen them as his people.

Palestine had been conquered many times by neighbouring countries before the Romans came. But the Jews had never lost their faith that one day, as the prophet had told them, a great ruler, a Messiah, would come to save them.

In Palestine, in the hills of Galilee, was the small town of Nazareth. During the reign of Emperor Augustus, a young woman, called Mary, lived there.

She was engaged to be married to a carpenter, called Joseph, who also lived in Nazareth. Joseph could trace his ancestors back to King David.

2

One day, God's messenger, the angel Gabriel, appeared to Mary. He said to her "Do not be afraid. I have been sent by God to tell you that you will have a son and you must call him Jesus. He will be great and he will be called the Son of the Most High."

Mary said, "But it is not possible. I am not yet married." Gabriel said, "The Holy Spirit will come on you and God's power will rest on you and your baby will be called holy, the Son of God." Mary bowed her head, "I am God's servant," she said. "I will do as he wishes."

Joseph was a good man. When he found that Mary was going to have a baby, he did not think it would be right to marry her and wanted to break off the engagement. But that night, he had a dream. In it an angel said to him;

"Joseph, do not be afraid to marry Mary, for that which is conceived in her is of the Holy Spirit. She is to give birth to a son and his name will be Jesus, the Son of God, and he will save people from their sins."

Next morning, when Joseph woke up, he remembered what the angel had told him and he started to make the arrangements for the wedding.

On the day of the wedding, Joseph put on his best clothes and went to Mary's house. He met the bridesmaids and he, Mary, her parents and their friends, walked in a solemn procession to his house. There they all had a great feast.

Some months later, Emperor Augustus, who lived far away in Rome, wanted to make sure that everyone in Palestine was paying the right amount of tax.

He made a new law which ordered every man in the country to return to the town where he had been born and put his name on the list of tax payers.

Roman soldiers nailed up notices in all the towns and villages throughout Palestine, telling the people what they must do. Any man who did not obey this order would be arrested by the soldiers and severely punished.

When Joseph read the notice, he went home to tell Mary, who was expecting her baby to be born quite soon now. "We must go to Bethlehem where I was born," he said, "so that I can sign the tax register there."

Joseph and Mary set out for Bethlehem with their donkey loaded with food, clothes and blankets. The town was about four days' journey over the hills to the south of Nazareth in Judea, and they stopped each night at inns along the road.

As they came within sight of Bethlehem, they were joined by more and more travellers going the same way.

When they reached the town in the evening, Joseph went to the nearest inn and asked for a room. But the inn keeper told him that his inn was already full.

Bethlehem was crowded with visitors and people from the surrounding hills and valleys who had come to register, so all his rooms were taken.

At the second inn, Joseph was given the same answer, and at the third inn.

Joseph knew that Mary's baby would be born very soon. He begged the inn keeper to find them somewhere to stay. "My wife is expecting a baby and is very tired after our long journey," he said. "Have you not even one small room where she could sleep?"

The inn keeper shook his head. "I am sorry," he said. "There are so many visitors in Bethlehem tonight, every room in my inn is full."

But then he added, pointing to the back of the inn, "I have a stable over there. It is quite clean. You may spend the night there if you wish."

Joseph wrapped his cloak round Mary, for the night was cold, and led her to the stable. He cleared out a stall and put fresh straw down on the floor.

There, during the night, with only Joseph to look after her, Mary gave birth to her son. She wrapped him up and laid him in a manger full of hay.

That same night, a group of shepherds sat round their camp fire on a hill above Bethlehem. They were guarding their flocks of sheep and lambs.

Suddenly, an angel sent by God stood in front of them, lighting up the ground all round them.

At first the shepherds were very frightened. But the angel said, "Do not be afraid. I have come with good news for you. Tonight the Son of God was born in Bethlehem. He is lying in a manger in a stable."

Around the angel, appeared many more angels, who sang the praises of God;

"Glory to God in highest Heaven, and on earth, peace among all men who love God."

The shepherds were overjoyed and excited because the angel had told them that the Messiah, the Saviour, who had been promised by the prophets for so long, had at last been born.

One stood up and said, "We must go to Bethlehem at once and look for this child." And they set off to walk through the star-lit night to the town.

When the shepherds reached the stable, they looked in wonder at the baby lying in the manger. It was exactly as the angel had told them. Quietly they knelt down on the straw in front of the manger and one offered a lamb as a gift.

The shepherds told Joseph and Mary what the angel had said and that they had come to Bethlehem to find the baby who would be their Saviour. Then they left to go back to their sheep.

On their way, the shepherds told everyone they met the good news of the birth of the Son of God. Soon the whole town had heard and rejoiced with the shepherds.

In the stable, Mary gazed at her baby son and thought about what the angel had told the shepherds. And she wondered what this message meant.

The shepherds were not the only people who knew of the birth of Jesus. Far away in another country, there were Wise Men who studied the stars. One night, they saw a new star, brighter than all the others, and they knew it must have a special meaning.

They studied all their scrolls about the stars to try to find out what this brilliant star could mean. At last, one of them said excitedly, "Listen," and began to read, "Whenever a bright new star appears in the sky, a mighty ruler has been born."

The Wise Men decided to go in search for this ruler and to take him royal gifts.

By following the star which shone in the night sky, they reached Jerusalem.

11

When King Herod heard that Wise Men from another country had arrived in Jerusalem and were looking for a new King of the Jews, he was angry and frightened. "I am the King of the Jews," he thought. "I must find out who this new King is."

He called all his priests and scholars and told them to search the ancient writings for information about a great ruler who would be born to reign over the people of God.

The priests and scholars went away to study their scrolls. At last, one discovered that, many years earlier, the prophet Micah had foretold that a leader of the people of Israel would be born in Bethlehem.

They hurried back to King Herod and told him what they had found. Herod listened carefully as a priest read out what the prophet had said. Then he sent a servant to ask the Wise Men to come to the Palace.

King Herod was a cunning man and wanted to find out more about this new King. After offering the Wise Men food and wine, he asked them how long ago they had first seen this new bright star.

"My priests and scholars tell me that the King will be born in Bethlehem," he said. "Go and search for the baby, and if you find him, come back and tell me, so that I also may honour him."

Secretly Herod was planning to have the baby killed, once he had found out from the Wise Men where this King was.

The Wise Men, not suspecting Herod's treachery, agreed to do as he asked and set out from Jerusalem.

They travelled along the road to Bethlehem with the bright star still in the night sky ahead of them.

As they reached the town, it seemed to stop above a certain place, and they knew that their long journey was over.

When they found the place, the Wise Men got off their camels and went in. Seeing Jesus, with his mother, Mary, they knelt down in front of him.

When they had offered the gifts they had brought from their own country — gold, frankincense and myrrh — they stood up and quietly left the stable.

Camping that night near Bethlehem, they soon fell asleep round their fire. But during the night, each one dreamt that the angel of God appeared to him.

The angel warned them that Herod wanted to kill Jesus. So the Wise Men did not go back to Jerusalem but went to their own country by a different road.

When Jesus was eight days old, Mary and Joseph left Bethlehem and went to the Temple in Jerusalem. Here the baby was circumcised, which was the Jewish custom. At the same time, the priest officially gave him the name of Jesus.

Then they set off for their home in Nazareth. But on the way, Joseph had a dream in which an angel said to him, "Take the child and escape to Egypt, for Herod will search for him to kill him." Mary and Joseph set off at once.

In Jerusalem, Herod waited for the Wise Men to return but as the days passed, he grew more and more suspicious. He did not know whether they had found the child. "Why have they not come back?" he asked angrily.

Herod called the Captain of the army. "Take a company of soldiers to Bethlehem," he ordered. "Go into every house and when you find a baby boy of two years old or younger, kill him!"

At the King's command, the soldiers marched to Bethlehem and searched the town, killing all the baby boys without mercy. But, by this time, Mary, Joseph and Jesus were safe in Egypt.

Some time later, Joseph had another dream. In it, the angel said, "Joseph, Herod is dead. It is now safe for you to take Mary and Jesus back to Nazareth."

Reaching home at last, they were welcomed by their relatives and friends. They settled into their house and Joseph worked again as a carpenter.

This is the sort of house Mary and Joseph lived in when they came back to Nazareth. The walls were made of mud and straw bricks and it had a flat roof.

There was only one room with very small windows. The animals were kept in the front near the door, and the family lived on a platform at the back.

One of the most important household possessions was the grinding mill. It was made of two round stones and used to grind corn into flour to make bread.

The large stone on the bottom had a spike in the middle which fitted into a hole in the top stone. Corn was poured through the hole, the top stone was turned and the corn was ground to flour between the two stones.

Most poor families had only a few other possessions, such as a wooden chest for clothes, some stools, cooking pots, and bowls for serving food.

Everyone slept on thin mattresses on the floor. These were rolled up each morning and stored on wooden shelves fixed to the walls.

Water was stored in porous clay pots to keep it cool. Olive oil was kept in jars which were glazed on the inside to stop the oil seeping out.

A lamp, full of olive oil, stood on a tripod. It burned all the time because no one slept in the dark and even during the day, the house was dark inside.

In good weather, most families cooked outside on charcoal fires, and baked flat loaves of bread in clay ovens.

In bad weather, they lit a fire inside the house but as there was no chimney, the room soon filled with smoke.

A small case containing a tiny scroll of parchment was fixed to the right-hand door post of every Jewish house. This was called the Mezuzah. Some verses from the Bible, called the "Shema" were written on the scroll.

Jesus, like all Jews, was taught to touch the Mezuzah and kiss his fingers every time he went in and out. This reminded him of God's presence and his duty to keep God's commandments at all times, inside and outside the house.

When he was six, Jesus went to school in the synagogue every morning. He had to learn the Hebrew alphabet and many passages from the Bible, until he could recite them by heart.

The Rabbi, the teacher, also taught his pupils the history of the Jews. And from the age of ten until he was fifteen, Jesus studied the sacred Law and learnt all the religious ceremonies and festivals.

All Jews kept every seventh day as a day of rest when no one was allowed to work. This was called the Sabbath and it lasted from sunset on Friday evening until sunset on Saturday.

Mary, like the mothers of all Jewish families, reminded Joseph and Jesus that the Sabbath day had begun by lighting special candles. The family then sat down for prayers and a meal.

The Jews probably built their first synagogues when they settled in Palestine, after wandering for years in the desert on their way from Egypt.

By the time Jesus was born, they were used as places of worship, schools and as the centre of local government.

Most Jews went to their local synagogue every Sabbath day, but only the men and older boys were allowed into the main hall. Women and girls sat apart from the men, behind a screen.

Every synagogue had a cupboard or "Ark" where the scrolls of the Law were kept. These were the rules which set out how Jews should live, and what was right and wrong. The leaders sat in front of the Ark, facing the people.

The service was mainly of prayers and readings from the Scriptures. It began with a prayer called the "Shema": "Hear, O Israel, the Lord our God is one Lord; and you shall love the Lord your God with all your heart, and with all your soul, and with all your might."

The Scriptures were written in the Hebrew language. But as most Jews in Palestine at that time spoke Aramaic, an interpreter translated each verse and gave an explanation.

23

At the Feast of the Passover, every Jewish family sacrificed a lamb. This festival reminded them of the time when Moses and their ancestors were slaves in Egypt. To force the Egyptians to set them free, the Angel of God killed the eldest son of every Egyptian family, but spared the Jewish families.

They ate bitter-tasting herbs to remind them of their suffering and slavery in Egypt. They baked flat, unleavened bread, which were loaves made without yeast, to remind them that they left Egypt very hurriedly; and drank a little salt water to remind them of how they crossed the Red Sea.

The Feast of Pentecost was held at the start of the grain harvest when the first sheaves were cut in the fields. This was fifty days, or seven weeks and one day, after the Feast of the Passover.

Pentecost was a time of happiness. The priests made sacrifices, and offerings of wheat were taken to the synagogues. Everyone gave thanks to God for giving them a another grain harvest.

The Feast of Yom Kippur was held in the autumn and lasted for ten days. During the first two days, Jews went to the synagogue to pray for forgiveness of their sins committed over the past year, and for health and happiness in the coming year.

The Rabbi wore a white linen robe as a sign of purity and blew a trumpet, called a shofar, made of a ram's horn to remind the people that they must repent. The last day was called the Day of Atonement, which meant "At-one" with God.

The Feast of Tabernacles was the happiest of all the Jewish festivals, and took place in the autumn when the fruit had been harvested. People built huts or tents in their gardens or on the flat roofs of their houses and camped in them.

The shelters were decorated with fruit and flowers, and covered with leaves and branches so that they could see the stars through them. This reminded the Jews of the time when their ancestors wandered with Moses in the desert.

Villages, like Nazareth where Jesus grew up, always had a spring or well nearby, because everyone needed water for drinking, cooking and washing, for their animals, and for watering crops.

Women came to the village well, carrying heavy water pots on their heads or shoulders. It was a favourite place to gossip and exchange news.

Most of the men who lived in Nazareth worked in the fields, growing food and looking after their sheep and goats.

It was a hard life because most of the fields were dry and stony and much of the land was mountainous. There was always the danger that locusts would eat the crops and that wild animals, such as lions, wolves and hyenas, would attack the animals.

The men grew grain which was ground into flour, grapes for making wine, and olives which were pressed for oil for cooking and for burning in lamps. Some farmers grew vegetables and fruit, such as figs and dates, and flax which was spun and woven to make linen cloth.

Shepherds looked after their flocks of sheep and goats, protecting them from wild animals, and moving them on each day to find grass and herbs to eat.

Craftsmen in the village earned food and money from the things they made. Dyers and weavers turned wool and flax into blankets and clothes. Potters made bowls and jars; blacksmiths and carpenters made tools and furniture.

Women ground corn and baked bread; they fetched water and worked in the fields, especially at harvest time.

Children also had to work, helping their families, but there was always time for Jesus to play with his friends.

When Jewish boys were thirteen years old, they became Bar-Mitzvah, which means a "Son of the Law". At that age, they were considered to be men and to be able to tell the difference between right and wrong. Each mother gave her son a cloak with fringes, called a Talith.

When Jesus was twelve, before his Bar-Mitzvah, Joseph and Mary took him to Jerusalem to celebrate the Feast of the Passover. They went with a party of other families from Nazareth as it was dangerous to travel alone on the roads because of gangs of robbers.

The journey took four days. At night they camped out in the open and ate their evening meals in family groups round their camp fires.

When they went into Jerusalem through one of the main gates in the city walls, they joined many other parties from the surrounding towns and villages.

In the Temple courtyard, the father of each family bought a lamb to be sacrificed and offered to God. This reminded the Jews that when they were slaves in Egypt, it was the blood of a lamb smeared on the doorpost of each house that made the Angel of God "pass over" and spare the eldest son.

When the Feast of the Passover had ended, the visitors from Nazareth gathered up their belongings and, early in the morning, set off for home through the crowded streets of Jerusalem.

At the end of the first day, they stopped and set up camp for the night. The donkeys were fed and watered; the men put up their tents and the women lit fires to cook the evening meal.

When the food was ready, Mary asked Joseph to tell Jesus to come and eat. Joseph went round the other tents, asking all Jesus' friends where he was. But they said that they had not seen Jesus at all that day.

Joseph and Mary were horrified when they realized that they had left Jesus behind in Jerusalem and went back at once to to look for him. They searched all the streets and asked everyone they met but they could not find Jesus.

After three days, when they despaired of finding him, Joseph said, "There is only one place we haven't looked and that is the Temple. If he is not there, I don't know what we shall do."

So they searched all round the Temple and in the Temple courtyard.

As they passed an open doorway leading to one of the council chambers, they heard a discussion going on.

Peeping in, they were astonished to see Jesus sitting with the Temple teachers, listening intently to their learned discussions. The teachers were amazed that he asked such intelligent questions and understood everything they said.

Joseph went into the room and asked the teachers if he too might speak to Jesus. "My Son," he said, "why have you treated us like this. Your mother and I have been terribly worried, and have been searching everywhere for you."

Jesus said he was sorry for causing so much trouble. Then he added, "But you need not have spent three days looking for me. Surely you should have guessed that I would be in the Temple, which is my Father's house."

Joseph and Mary did not understand what Jesus meant. But Mary remembered what he said and often thought about it.

They went home to Nazareth and Jesus lived there until the time came for him to travel the country, teaching people about God.